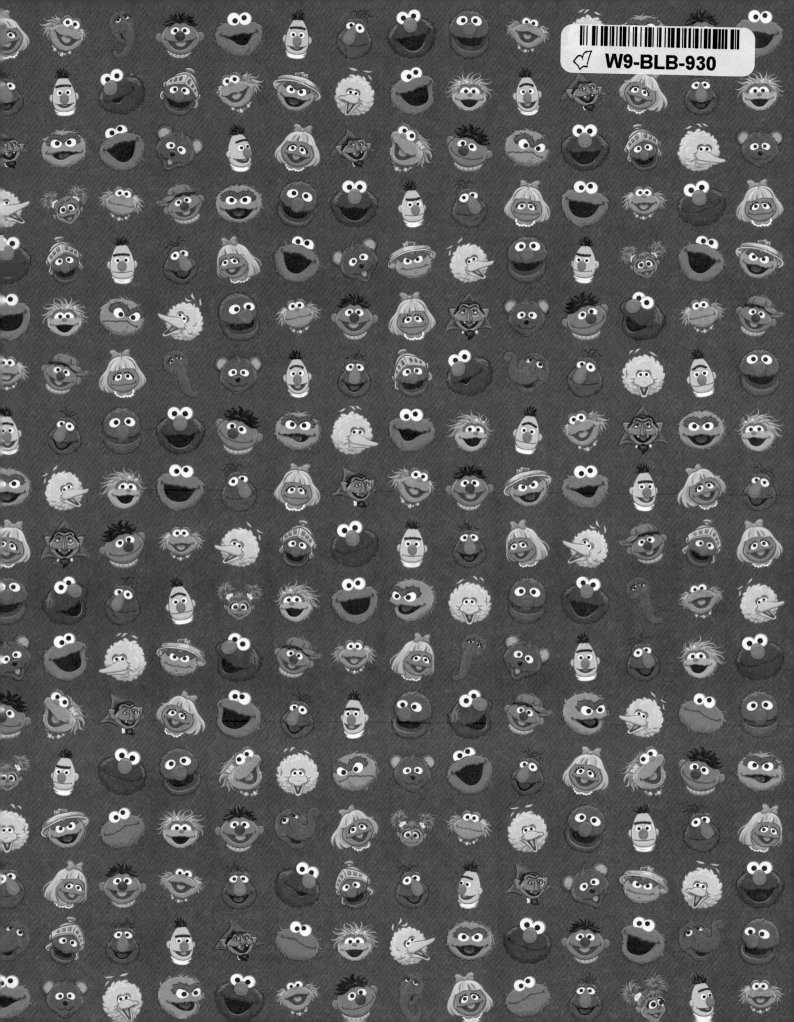

W9-BLB-930

123 SESAME STREET®

Animal Crafts

First published by Parragon in 2009

Parragon
Queen Street House
4 Queen Street
Bath BA1 1HE, UK

"Sesame Workshop"®, "Sesame Street"®, and associated
characters, trademarks, and design elements are owned and
licensed by Sesame Workshop. © 2009 Sesame Workshop.
All Rights Reserved.

No part of this publication may be reproduced, stored in a
retrieval system or transmitted, in any form or by any means,
electronic, mechanical, photocopying, recording or otherwise,
without the prior permission of the copyright holder.

ISBN 978-1-4075-7196-6

Printed in China

SESAME STREET

123

Animal Crafts

PaRragon

Bath · New York · Singapore · Hong Kong · Cologne · Delhi · Melbourne

TIPS FOR SUCCESS

Prepare your space

Cover your workspace with newspaper or a plastic or paper tablecloth. Make sure you and your children are wearing clothes (including shoes!) that you don't mind becoming spattered with food, paint, or glue. But relax! You'll never completely avoid mess; in fact, it's part of the fun!

Wash your hands

Wash your hands (and your child's hands) before starting a new project, and clean up as you go along. Clean hands make for clean crafts! Remember to wash your hands afterward, too, using soap and warm water to get off any of the remaining materials.

Follow steps carefully

Follow each step carefully, and in the sequence in which it appears. We've tested all the projects; we know they work, and we want them to work for you, too. Also, ask your children, if they are old enough, to read along with you as you work through the steps. For a younger child, you can direct her to look at the pictures on the page to try to guess what the next step is.

Measure precisely

If a project gives you measurements, use your ruler, T-square, measuring cups, or measuring spoons to make sure you measure as accurately as you can. Sometimes the success of the project may depend on it. Also, this is a great opportunity to teach measuring techniques to your child.

Be patient

You may need to wait while something bakes or leave paint, glue, or clay to dry, sometimes for a few hours or even overnight. Encourage your child to be patient as well; explain to her why she must wait, and, if possible, find ways to entertain her as you are waiting. For example you can show her how long you have to wait by pointing out the time on a clock.

Clean up

When you've finished your project, clean up any mess. Store all the materials together so that they are ready for the next time you want to craft. Ask your child to help.

Sand butterfly

Elmo is a very busy monster. Elmo is painting a butterfly picture using sand. What will you paint with sand?

You will need

- 8 x 11 inch sheets of cardboard
- 8 x 11 inch sheets of white paper
- Pencil
- Black felt-tip pen
- Scissors
- $11\frac{3}{4} \times 16\frac{1}{2}$ inch sheet scrap paper
- White glue and brush
- Colored sand: red, orange, yellow, blue, green
- Teaspoon

1

To make a butterfly, fold the white paper and draw half of its shape on one side. Cut it out. Unfold the shape and put it on the cardboard at an angle.

2

Use the black felt-tip pen to draw around the outline. Add butterfly markings, matching the pattern on each wing.

3

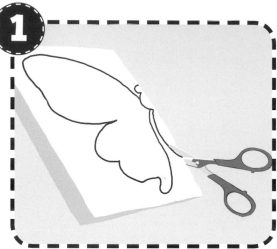

Place the scrap paper under the cardboard. Paste a thin layer of white glue over the butterfly's body and head only.

Scoop some yellow sand into the spoon and sprinkle over the glued area. Lift the picture and gently tap the spare sand onto the scrap paper. Carefully pour the sand back into its container.

Continue gluing and sprinkling until you've finished your picture.

It is I, Grover, your furry adorable globe trotter. I traveled all the way to Italy. Did you know "farfalle" is butterfly-shaped pasta?

Bird feeder

Recycling is a good way to use old things in a new way. For example, turn an old juice carton into a bird feeder.

You will need

- Empty, rinsed-out juice carton with a nozzle
- Sandpaper
- Scissors
- Acrylic paints
- Paintbrush
- Bird seed
- Garden wire
- Mesh netting bag
- Varnish

1

Rub the outside of the carton with sandpaper until it's rough. Cut out a rectangular hole on the side facing away from the nozzle.

kids 2

Paint the carton all over in one color. This one is brown to look like tree bark.

kids 3

After the paint is dry, add different shades and colors. This one has knots and vines, just like bark.

Add leaves or other decorations in a different color. When you've finished painting, add a coat of varnish to help protect the feeder during cold and wet months.

5

Fill the mesh netting bag with birdseed, then push it through the rectangular hole in the feeder. Remove the nozzle, then pull the top of the bag through the spout. Next, thread wire through the top of the bag and twist the ends together. Hang the feeder up outside.

That's so magic—the old juice carton is now a bird feeder!

Slithery snail pots

These smiling snails look great and they can store a special surprise. You can hide your tiny treasures under their shell!

You will need

- 5 ounces air-drying clay cut in half
- Plastic knife
- 1 purple pipe cleaner
- Scissors
- Toothpick
- Acrylic paints: red, blue, yellow, purple, black, white
- Paintbrush

1

Roll a ¾-inch ball and 2 tiny balls from half of the clay. Stick the 2 tiny balls onto the larger ball. Cut 2 short pieces of pipe cleaner and push them into the larger ball.

2

With the rest of the clay from the first half, make a tapered oval shape. Use your thumbs to create an indent in the middle. Stick the head to the untapered end.

3

Roll the other half of clay into a ball and shape into a hollow shell shape. Check it fits the base of your model. Add a spiral on each side using the toothpick. Let dry overnight.

Paint the head, the eyes, and the base any color you like.

Paint the shell and outline the spiral. Add a smiling mouth and paint on pupils for the eyes.

What super treasures will you keep inside your secret snail?

For a grasshopper pot, make a long base and lid and push 6 green pipe-cleaner legs into the base. Paint the pot bright green all over and add red spots.

Pet photo frame

If you like animals as much as Elmo does, make this cute frame for a picture of your favorite pet or animal.

You will need

- 4 cardboard strips 6 x 1 inch
- 12 Popsicle sticks
- Cardboard (to fit photo)
- 2 different-sized pens (any kind)
- Acrylic paint
- Photo of pet or favorite animal
- Scissors
- Clear adhesive tape

1

Paint the Popsicle sticks and let dry (or use colored ones).

2

Glue 3 Popsicle sticks onto each cardboard strip, leaving about an inch gap at both ends. Then glue the ends of the cardboard strips together into a frame shape.

3

Dip the end of the largest pen into the paint and press down around the frame. Then use the smaller pen to add circles to complete the paw prints.

4

Tape a photo of your pet into the frame then cover the back with a piece of cardboard.

This makes a great gift. I'm going to give mine to my Mommy.

Shell plant pot

The next time you're at the beach, pick up a handful of seashells, or ask your mommy to buy some at a craft store. They make a plain plant pot magic!

You will need

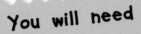

- ★ Seashells
- ★ Acrylic paint
- ★ Paintbrushes
- ★ Clean plant pot (plastic or ceramic)
- ★ White glue and brush

1 Paint some shells in bright colors. Let dry. Paint leaves on the side of a plant pot. Let dry.

2 Glue the shells onto the plant pot. Let the glue dry.

3 Paint snail bodies coming out from under the shells, or create other designs you like around the shells and on the pot.

4

Paint faces and antennae onto the snails, or add other patterns. Let dry. Now add a plant to your pot.

Elmo loves going to the beach and feeling the water splash across his feet! What kind of creatures can you find in the sea?

kitty photo album

This collage photo album will make a purr-fect present for your favorite cat lover!

1

Pile together the 6 sheets of colored cardboard with the cover sheet on top. Punch 2 holes on the left-hand side.

You will need

- 6 sheets 8½ x 11 inches, colored cardboard
- Scraps of card in orange, white, pink, green, black, and blue
- Hole punch
- Pinking shears
- White glue and brush
- 3-foot long piece of green cord

kids

2

Using the pinking shears cut a strip from each of the card scraps. Arrange them to make a border on the cover and glue in place.

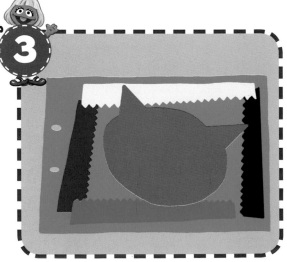

kids

3

Draw and cut out a large cat face from orange cardboard. Glue it on the cover, overlapping the borders as shown.

Draw and cut out the cat's oval white eyes with green and black pupils. Cut out a pink nose, mouth, some ears, and black whiskers. Arrange these on the face and glue them in place.

Thread the length of cord through the holes, starting from the back and including all the pages. Tie in a bow at the front. Knot the ends of the cord to stop them from fraying.

Instead of an orange kitty, make a photo album with a picture of your pet on the front. Or, just make a pretty design any way you wish!

Pebble porcupines

Elmo likes making animals from smooth beach pebbles. Elmo is painting pebble porcupines today. What will you paint?

You will need

- 1 large and 2 small smooth stones
- Acrylic paints
- Medium and small paintbrushes
- Clear varnish

Kids

1

Wash and dry the stones. Paint them the color of the animal you want to make. Paint an extra coat if you need to. Let dry.

Asking questions is a good way to find out about something you want to know. Like... what is a porcupine? You'll find the answer in step 2.

2

Porcupines are animals with spiky spines or quills. To make pebble porcupines, paint the pebbles gray, let dry, then paint on black bristles.

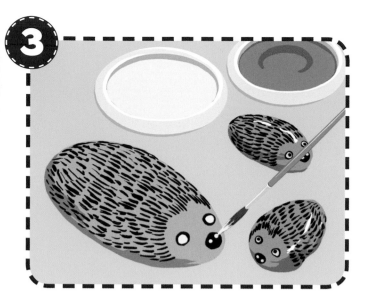

Now add a nose and two eyes, then paint your other pebbles.

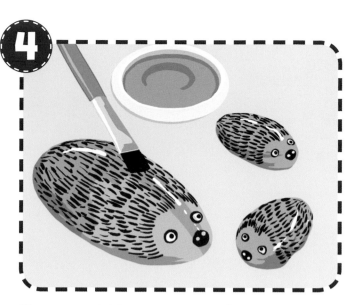

If your pebbles are going to live outside on your doorstep or your backyard, give them all a coat of clear varnish.

Elmo has made a scaly fish friend for Dorothy from this long pebble. Elmo is looking in his animal book to see what other creatures he can make from his pebbles.

Leaf creatures

These leaf creatures look so funny and they're easy to make. You just need some leaves and some imagination.

1

Choose a large dried leaf and glue it onto the piece of cardboard.

You will need

- ✯ Various dried leaves
- ✯ Piece of cardboard (any color)
- ✯ White glue and brush
- ✯ Colored pens
- ✯ Colored paper
- ✯ Scissors
- ✯ Wobbly eyes, or colored dot stickers

2

Choose some smaller leaves and stick them to the cardboard for hands, feet, and ears. Draw lines between the small leaves and the big leaf for arms and legs.

3

Stick wobbly eyes onto the leaf and add a smile shape cut from the colored paper.

4

Make more leaf creatures using different kinds of leaves. Make funny faces, like 3 eyes or curly antennae.

Elmo loves making leaf creatures best. Elmo is going to make up names for these leaf creatures. Do you want to try too?

Tiger paws

Turn old tissue boxes into wild feet, like these tiger paws—maybe even your favorite monster's feet from Sesame Street.

You will need

- 2 empty tissue boxes
- Acrylic paints
- Paintbrush and old sponge
- Black funky foam
- 10 double-sided adhesive tabs or tape
- Scissors
- White glue and brush

1

To make tiger feet paint the top and sides of the tissue boxes yellow, then let dry.

2

Dip a dry sponge in orange paint and dab it all over the boxes. Let dry.

3

Paint black stripes all over the boxes. Let dry.

4

Cut out claws from the black foam. Glue them onto the box using double-sided adhesive tabs on top.

Hey everybody. My feet are large and furry. What kind of feet will you make?

Fishy glitter globe

This is a great way to use an old jar. Fill it with glittery water, paint on your favorite fish, like Dorothy, and shake up a storm!

You will need

- Empty round jar and lid
- Seashells (optional)
- All-purpose waterproof glue
- Black relief outliner glass paint
- Glass paints: red, orange, green
- Paintbrush
- Water
- Glycerine
- Blue glitter

kids 1

Arrange shells on the inside of the jar lid. Glue them to the lid and let dry.

2

Turn the jar upside down and, using the black relief paint, draw the outline of fish and seaweed. Let dry.

3

Using the glass paints and brush, color in the seaweed and fish, blending the paints together. Let dry.

Fill the jar with water. Add a teaspoon of glitter and a few drops of glycerine.

Put a line of glue around the lid and screw it tightly to the top of the jar. Let dry overnight.

Glycerine is great! It makes the water thicker, so when you shake the jar, the glitter falls slowly to the bottom. You can buy it in the home-baking department of your supermarket.

Shake the jar and place it upside down to give your fish a glittery sea to swim in.

Mini farmyard

Make your own farmyard scene of cute sheep and clucking chickens with oven-drying clay. Ask an adult to help you bake them.

kids 1

For the hens' bodies, roll and shape the brown clay into simple crescent shapes.

You will need

❧ Oven-bake clay: brown, red, yellow, white, black, green

Elmo found out that if you wet the edges of the clay pieces a little bit, they stick together better.

2

Roll a small lump of red clay and press it flat with your thumb. Stick it to one end of the body. Add a small yellow cone shape for the beak. Add a small red blob underneath for the wattle.

kids 3

Add tiny black blobs of clay for eyes. Make a small ball from the green clay and flatten the bottom. Place the hen on top and push it down firmly to stick it in place.

For the sheep, mold a ball of white clay into an oval shape for the body. Make a head, 2 ears, and 4 legs out of the black clay.

Stick the head, ears, and legs to the sheep's body. Bake all the animals in the oven, following the manufacturer's instructions.

These animuls live on a farm. Grouches prefer living in trash cans though.

Bottle-top snake

Use the tops of plastic soda bottles to make a super, slithery snake. Ask an adult to save you the two wine corks you need.

You will need

- Champagne-style cork
- Wine cork
- Green acrylic paint and brush
- Plastic bottle tops: 30 green, a few red and white
- Old ballpoint pen
- 3 small screw eyes
- 24-inch piece of string
- Small bell
- 2 wobbly eyes
- Scrap of red felt
- Scissors
- White glue and brush

kids

1

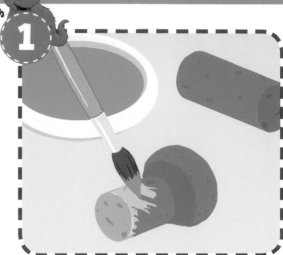

Paint both corks all over with the green acrylic paint. Let dry.

2

Using the old ballpoint pen, make a hole in the middle of each of the bottle tops.

3

Screw one eye into the top of the champagne cork. Add the bell to another screw eye, and screw this and the remaining eye into each end of the wine cork.

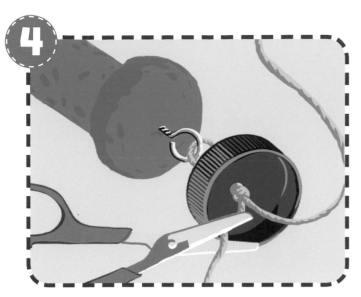

Thread one end of the string through the bottom of a green bottle top. Now thread it through the champagne cork's screw eye and back through the bottle top. Make a knot and trim one end only.

5

Thread all the bottle tops onto the string, keeping them all facing the same way around. Finish by tying the string to the screw eye on the wine cork.

6

Glue the wobbly eyes in place. Cut a thin forked tongue from the red felt and use the pen to poke it into the cork.

Snakes use their tongues to "taste" the air. This tells them if food is nearby. Snakes can be dangerous so if you see one, go and tell a grown-up right away and don't touch!

Cress caterpillar

Watercress only takes a few days to grow and it tastes great in salads and sandwiches, too. Elmo loves watercress!

You will need

- 5 egg shells
- Nail scissors
- Paints: green, red, black
- Wobbly eyes
- Paintbrush
- White glue and brush
- Packet of watercress seeds
- Cotton batting
- Red pipe cleaner
- Water

1

Take 5 clean, empty egg shells with their tops cut off. Trim the top of the egg shells with nail scissors to make them smooth.

2

Paint the shells green. Glue wobbly eyes on one shell and paint a mouth. Put all the shells in an egg carton to dry.

kids 3

Once dry, place some cotton batting in the bottom of each shell. Add 1 teaspoon of watercress seeds and a spoonful of water to each shell.

Cut up a cardboard egg carton to make five little dishes. Paint them green and glue them together in a wiggly line.

Place an egg shell in each dish, with the face at the front. Make antennas by twisting a pipe cleaner into spirals at both ends, fold it in half, then push it into the shell with the face.

Add a little water every other day. Within a week, the watercress will grow. Then you can wash and eat it. I'm going to make a cress salad for my good friend, Snuffy.

INDEX

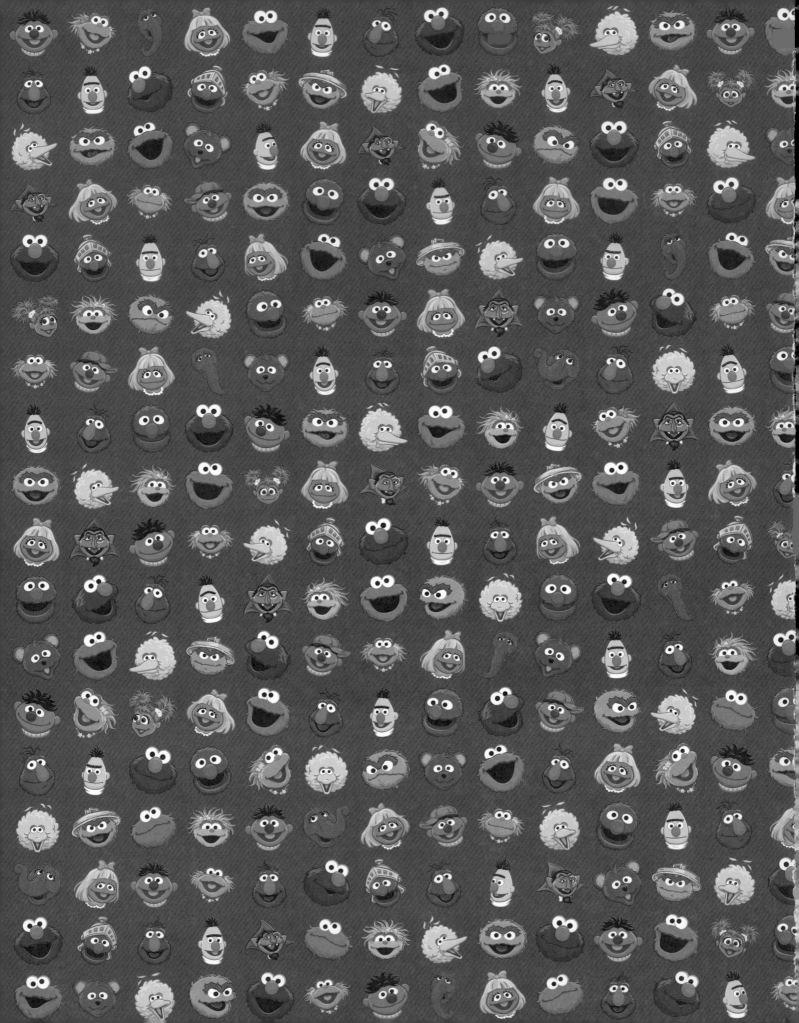